GIRL BAND

JANET HOGGARTH

The Chicken House
An Egmont joint venture

She's a Bright New Star

Everyone wants to be a popstar! Just like those talent shows on TV - we all dream of being discovered. Then we can appear in front of millions of fans, while our friends drool and our teachers HAVE to give those interviews where they say: "Well, we always knew she was something special!"

HUH, like they really noticed!

But real Stars get going early - Mandy Moore started by "jumping up and down on my bed singing" and appearing at summer camp shows at 9! And Christina Aguilera was discovered when she was 8 on a show called *Star Search,* then appeared on America's *Mickey Mouse Club* when she was 12, with another girl in her backing group called Britney. . .

And of course our own Billie Piper was another early starter - leaving school and going straight on to *Top of the Pops!*

Now you can join the fun too! Find out the real deal on everything you need to know about getting together your own Girl Band, and meet KandyFloz, the girls to show you how!

To my sisters, Joanna and Katie,
who know how to party like
a real girl band!

© The Chicken House 2001
Text © Janet Hoggarth 2001
Illustrations © Sarah Symonds 2001

First published in Great Britain in 2001
The Chicken House
2, Palmer Street
Frome
Somerset
BA11 1DS

Cover and text design by Mandy Sherliker
Printed and bound in Great Britain

British Library Cataloguing in Publication data available.

ISBN 1-903434-25-4

Contents

1.
Wannabe

Hey – we saw you! Singing into your hairbrush thinking no one could see you. You were pretty good, actually, not bad for someone who dances like an electrocuted spider. You need some lessons there, girl! That's why we're here – to show you the way. We know you wanna sing, wanna dance, but why not do it with some friends? Why not think of a name, get some songs together, do some jiggy moves on the dance floor – form a GIRL BAND!

So how come *we* know so much? Well, you did ask. We are KandyFloz, the best and funkiest, maddest and baddest, grooviest and smoothest band to come along in… well, since girl bands began. You always need to be different, and we are cos we have the fastest rapper in the world – MotorMouth LaydeeB – who makes us laugh with her awesome speed. But don't cross her, or you might end up a quivering wreck – she has a tongue as sharp as a viper's bite! It's time to come and say hi to us, your girl band guides – we'll be showing you how to get it together as the coolest chicks on the block.

Skye

Age: 14

Star sign: Gemini

Pets: her little brother

Loves: pizza, running, singing, any dance music, art, make-up and the movies

Loathes: fish, Backstreet Boys and Furbies

Most embarrassing moment: "My leotard ripping in a school gymnastic display!"

Motto: Get there first before anyone else.

Kym

Age: 14

Star sign: Aries

Pets: canary, lizard, two fish and a
hamster called Mr Pig

Loves: popcorn, Destiny's Child, dancing,
sunshine, holidays and her mum

Loathes: rain ("it makes my hair go frizzy!"),
all rock music, meat and peas

Most embarrassing moment:
"Wetting my pants from laughing so much in a
maths lesson!"

Motto: Go for it!

Fazza

Age: 13

Star sign: Capricorn

Pets: a dog called Dave
(for real - Dave the dog!)

Loves: Madonna, her dog, her family,
chocolate, singing and peanut butter

Loathes: burger bars, jazz music, cauliflower
("gross!"), sunburn and boys who are jerks!

Most embarrassing moment: "Treading
in dog doo and walking
it through the whole school!"

Motto: Just be happy!

MMLaydeeB

Age: 15

Star sign: Sagittarius

Pets: No way! They are for dweebs

Loves: fashion, writing, Reece's Peanut Cups, going out, Eminem and her trendy sunglasses

Loathes: rude people, dark chocolate, eggs, Celine Dion, falling over ("I always do it!") and oranges

Most embarrassing moment: "Realising I had forgotten all the words to a song I was singing in the school play and having to get the script to manage it..."

Right – the book starts here! It's got everything you need to know from hair styles to stage shows, from funky diva clothes to manic make-up. If we can't make you look a million dollars by the end of this book, I promise I will give away my sunglasses.

And you know how much she loves those sunglasses! You girls had better be cooler than the all the boy bands put together.

That won't be hard!

GIRL BAND

2.
Step back in time

 I'm the resident expert on our favourite Girl Power performers. Take a trip with me and check out the icons through the mists of time – Girl Power didn't all start with the Spice Girls, you know. There were girl music sensations as far back as the time before dinosaurs... well, the 1930s.

The Stone Age

Gasp, shock, horror! Yes, the 1930s and 40s. But they didn't sing pop, no siree, it was good old Big Band music. The Andrews Sisters were the Destiny's Child of their day and were massssssssive during the Second World War. They were still going in the 1960s, singing fogey classics like *Jingle Bells* and *Underneath the Arches*. The UK's answer to the Andrews Sisters was the Beverly Sisters - they had their own TV show, like S Club 7, and they stormed the charts in the 1950s and 60s. Swing those pants!

Then came the 1960s! It was all change, all change! Girls were forming groups left, right and centre. And Motown was the coolest sound around. Thigh-length boots and mini-skirts ruled the skool...

The sixties, maaaan

The famous producer (well, ask your 'rents) Phil Spector gave us groups such as the Crystals (*Da Doo Ron Ron, Then He Kissed Me* – you *must* know those! Your old man will for sure!) and the Ronettes, who warbled mega hit *Be My Baby*. Another girlie act from the sixties was Martha and the Vandellas, whose hit, *Dancing in the Street*, was covered by ageing rockers Mick Jagger (or rather Mick Jowler) and David Bowie for the historic concert, Live Aid. Were your 'rents in the crowd? Gladys Knight and the Pips also dominated the charts throughout the sixties and seventies and well into the eighties. Go those Pips!

The Shirelles had probably the most well-known hit, *Will You Still Love Me Tomorrow*, but it's the Supremes who are the biggest-selling Girl Super Group EVER – even after all this time. Fronted by

Diana Ross, now a superstar in her own right, they stormed the charts with every release they made. The most famous was *Stop! In the Name of Love.*

Now you know you just wanna search out your 'rents', or even your old granny's records to listen to those original girl bands, dontcha? They got some banging tunes...

It happened first in the seventies...

Hehehehehehehehheeeee! The seventies – glitter, flares, platforms, satin hot pants – no, really, all this happened before we were born, but look at how little has changed! You just aren't anyone at the moment if you haven't got gold eye shadow. So slap it on and check out these superstars of the stompin' seventies.

The seventies was the disco decade but it didn't have as many girl groups as the sixties or even the next decade – the eighties. But there were a few who really stood out from the crowd as glitter queens. The Pointer Sisters strutted their stuff through the seventies and the eighties with a string of disco hits including *Jump (For My Love)* and *I'm So Excited.*

Joining them in sisterhood was Sister Sledge, famous for the disco classic *We Are Family*. Just watch all the wrinklies get up and dance to it when you go to your cousin's wedding. I bet this tune is the one that really gets them going! The Three Degrees were famous for being Prince Charles's favourite girl group in the seventies and even played at his thirtieth birthday party. Rock on, Charlie!

The biggest cheese of the seventies wasn't a girl band, but a girl-boy band. They have to have a mention because they're the influence behind beloved Brit bands such as S Club 7, Steps and US copycats Boys+Girls United, who are all big stars today. Of course, we're talking about ABBA! My heroes! ABBA from Sweden won the Eurovision Song Contest in 1974 with the now famous *Waterloo*. They were the supergroup of the decade with number one singles all over the world – *Dancing Queen, I Have a Dream* (covered by Westlife), *Mama Mia* – the list is endless. Without them, where would all those copycat groups be today?

Lace and crucifixes – the eighties...

This is where things start to get interesting. The eighties had the New Romantics – glitter, frilly shirts, big make-up – but that was just for the boys! Us ladies didn't want all that trash – we went for lace, fingerless gloves and big hair that looked like it had been superglued in a hurricane. Way to go...

Well, the eighties saw girls scale new heights and pave the way for the explosion of female performers in the nineties. Yeah! The Go-Go's were an American group who had hits mostly in the US. Singer Belinda Carlisle left the group to start a successful solo career with ditties *Heaven is a Place on Earth* and *We Want the Same Thing*. Another girl group to make waves was the Bangles. They had tons of hits, which I'm sure your olds have got stashed away in their dusty CD collection: *Walk Like an Egyptian* and *Eternal Flame*. Go and snoop!

The UK's biggest ever girl band till the Spices was Bananarama. With hair like backcombed mohair jumpers and scruffy clothes, they were like our big sisters. Their hits included *Cruel Summer* and *Shy Boy*. This threesome still managed to slam-dunk the charts with hits even after a member left and was replaced by a friend of the band.

If Bananarama were the sweets of the Brit scene, then Salt-N-Pepper were the savoury US girl rap duo. These girls had attitude and weren't afraid to show it! Originally telephone sales girls, they had hooooge hits with *Push It* and *Twist and Shout*.

We've just got to include someone else, even though she's not a girl group. She's had enough image changes, hairstyles, hit singles and various scandals for at least ten girl groups put together: Madonna! The Queen of Pop was responsible for the lace fingerless glove and crucifix craze of the eighties. Hmmm – was that a good thing? Her popularity endures as she is still the number one female performer ever, churning out hit after hit.

Another chameleon girlie performer who was big in the eighties but is still banging out records today is Janet Jackson. She released her first album at sixteen and with hit after hit in the eighties, she was a real contender for Queen of Pop, but that was already taken...

Snapping at the heels of Madonna were teen sensations Tiffany, who performed in shopping malls across the globe, and Debbie Gibson, who went on to make her name in theatre in the UK and US. These teen songstresses set the standard for the nineties and millennium obsession with finding younger and younger stars for the teen music market, either as groups or as solo performers...

All that spice...

 So, we are now in the time of our heroines. This was the decade of Girl Power and the time when us laydeees took over the charts before we'd even finished school. Awesome!

The start of the nineties saw Kylie Minogue, a former Australian soap star, dominate the UK charts. She'd had hits at the end of the eighties, but now she really made the big time. If Madonna is the Queen, surely Kylie is the Princess of Pop. She has made a big comeback today, and I know you can't stop tapping those Nikes to *Spinning Around*...

All went quiet on the girl front for a while. We had En Vogue and TLC (still going strong), but it was boy bands such as New Kids on the Block, Take That and Back Street Boys who ruled the charts. Yawn... But then one day, I turned on the radio and out came this sound, like nothing I had ever heard before. *Zigazig haaaaaaa* ... The Spice Girls! From then on we had Ginger telling us about Girl Power – sooooo cool. *Wannabe* stormed to number one across the world and the rest is history. Even when

Geri left to be a successful solo artist, the Spices kept charging on with those hits. Nothing could stop the wave of girl bands that was about to swamp the international charts. This is OUR time!

After the Spices came All Saints with *Never Ever* and best-selling albums, then B*Witched with *C'est La Vie*. After that a wave of teenage girl groups and girl-boy groups descended upon us. Wow! Now let me see, there's Billie Piper, the youngest girl to have a string of number one hits in Europe; Britney Spears, the biggest teen star of the moment; Christina Aguilera, Britney's rival; and S Club 7, brought to us by the ex-manager of the Spices. Also, Samantha Mumba, Steps (Abba soundalikes), Boys+Girls United, Girl Thing (apparently the next Big Thing in girl bands), Brandy and Monica (teen sensations stateside) and their counterparts in the UK, Cleopatra. There's Destiny's Child (the next big girl group), the Honeyz, obnoxious US duo Daphne and Celeste (they is scary, sisters!), Mandy More and Jessica Simpson and many, many more teen stars, too numerous to mention...

PSST! **Gossip** Britney nearly joined US girl band Innosense before she made it big.

Where will it end? Let's hope it doesn't. All these acts are dancing their way into the Millennium along with us, KandyFloz! Now you can see that girl bands are not a new phenomenon. But it isn't until now that we have made it BIG TIME and showed the world what Girl Power is all about. We rule!

GIRL BAND

26

3. Who do you think you are?

Well, you've seen the competition, past and present. Has it inspired you? It did me. I just know you chicas are gonna want to get it together as funky divas, sing those songs and slam-dunk the funk on the stage to all your fans. But first, you gotta have a name, dontcha?

Yeah! BUT before you even think about a name, do you and your posse have what it takes to be IN a girl band? Could you handle being away from home and always being on the road with no little corner of your own? Life's not always a bowl of cherries! Don't say I didn't warn you...

PSST! Gossip There's no escape from school, even when you top the charts! US teen sensation Mandy Moore does all her schoolwork over the Internet to keep up to date. ZZZzzz.

27

Are YOU girl band material?
Try this tough test:

1. How often do you need to see your closest buddies?

a. Every day – what else is school for?

b. As much as possible – at least every other day.

c. You're not bothered, as long as you can call them.

2. Could you handle long periods away from home?

a. Maybe, but you might get homesick.

b. If it meant you'd be a superstar, then you guess so.

c. Not yet, you like your home comforts too much.

3. Would you get all star-struck if you met a celeb?

a. Yes. You'd love it, but probably get really nervous.

b. No, not at all. They are human, aren't they?

c. Maybe at first, but then you'd have to snap out of it.

4. How much does your own space mean to you?

a. Everything. If you can't be on your own sometimes you go crazy.

b. Depends how you feel – sometimes it's important, but not always.

c. Not much. You hate being on your own anyway.

5. Could you perform even when you're not in the mood?

a. You guess, but you probably wouldn't be much good.

b. Of course! You are always in the mood!

c. No way. Sometimes you just want to go and watch TV.

PSST! Gossip Some advice from UK girl band, Cleopatra: "Don't be a 'genie in a bottle' like Christina Aguilera! Don't wait for someone else to change things, stand up for yourself! But don't be too harsh, or no one will respect you for it."

Did you pass go?

Results: 1. a 0 b 5 c 10   2. a 5 b 10 c 0   3. a 0 b 10 c 5
4. a 0 b 5 c 10   5. a 5 b 0 c 0

If you scored 0-15

Hmm. You're not sure, are you? You prefer chilling at home with your friends and family to buzzing round the country singing and dancing. There's plenty of time for playing the fame game later on, so don't sweat.

If you scored 20-30

You've definitely got potential for life as a girl band member but, right now, you are happy with your life as a normal kid. Just keep practising those dance moves and high notes!

If you scored 35-40

You've got all the makings of a chart-topper! Try to keep your feet on the ground while you whirl round in a rush of gigs and photo shoots. But remember to have fun and take time to chill, sister!

PSST! Gossip The UK's answer to Britney, Billie Piper, has had old school friends selling stories about her to the papers. That's what you have to put up with if you're famous. Still want to make it big?

 Do you think you've got what it takes to be in a girl band? Endless interviews, photo sessions, make-up calls, shows, no time to be yourself. Would you turn into an Ego-monster or be the Princess of Pop...

Pop or flop?

1. You are stuck in traffic on the way for a live TV show. It looks like you have no time for full make-up. Do you:

a. Have a major row with the driver, blaming him – you look foul without lippy!?

b. Plead with the make-up ladies when you get there to powder away your shiny nose?

c. Make-up isn't everything - your performance is what matters?

2. You are in an interview and get asked to comment about someone who has been bad-mouthing you. Do you:

a. Diss them too and say what a lowlife they are? If you can't beat 'em, join 'em!

b. Say they really hurt you and you think they are just jealous?

c. Don't say anything - you don't care what they say cos you know it's not true?

3. You do a photo spread for a magazine and are allowed to approve the pictures. Do you:

a. Get them to airbrush your face - you don't want people to see all your spots?

b. Choose one you like and say they are not allowed to use any of the others?

c. Let them choose - as long as you don't look too hideous, you're cool with that?

4. During a TV show performance, your trousers split, but there's no time to do a retake. Do you:

a. Demand a retake even though you know it will ruin

the time schedule of other acts?

b. Refuse to dance with rest of the band in case you look stupid, but carry on singing?

c. Try not to laugh but act like nothing's happened – you might make the headlines!

5. You have to revise for an exam, but have got an invite to a cool celeb party. Do you:

a. Go to the party, stupid! Who cares about exams, you're a pop star!

b. Revise like mad for a few hours and then go out, you need a break?

c. Stay in and study? You might not be a pop star for ever.

6. You are having dinner in a restaurant with your family and a fan wants to pose for a picture and have your autograph. Do you:

a. Get really angry and shout at them to go away? How dare they interrupt your meal!

b. Reluctantly sign the autograph, but say no to the picture – you are having a private night?

c. Pose for a pic and sign your napkin – you've always got time for fans?

7. It's your best friend's birthday and you are on tour with the girls. Did you:

a. Forget completely – you don't have time to remember things like that any more?

b. Remember at the last minute and ring her on the day to say her present's in the post?

c. Arrange for her to come to the show and take her out for a meal after the concert?

PSST! Gossip Irish teen star Samantha Mumba has this to say about fame: "It's crazy being recognized everywhere you go. People's attitudes towards you change; all of a sudden people want to do things for you. I don't like that. It's a little mad."

Are you beauty or the beast?

Mostly A's

Oh no! You are a pop brat! You're not too young to be locked in your bedroom with no supper, young lady. You'll not last long with that bad attitude!

Mostly B's

You manage quite well with the pressures of fame and a normal life. Sometimes you can be a bit of a madam, but only slightly. That Princess of Pop crown is almost yours.

MOSTLY C's

You are a true Princess. Britney looks like a wild child compared to you. You have your feet firmly on the ground and just wanna have fun. After all, isn't that what it's all about?

PSST! Gossip A Britney fan decided to brighten up dull physics lessons by creating a web site at www.britneyspears.ac.uk . As well as all the usual info, the site has Britney's Guide to Semiconductor Physics, using her curves to illustrate mathematical equations!

Name in one

Sisters, you should be well on the way to realising your potential as future stars and this is when you really have to get it together on the name front. Here are some ideas to help you come up with something stylish for your act.

Drop of a hat

Well, this sounds very obvious, but sooo easy. Gather your girlies around you and get chilling with some drinks and snacks and pens and paper. Now write words on pieces of paper that you think are inspiring or funky or funny – whatever! Use film titles, song titles, TV programmes. Try some of these:

Fresh ✳ Funky ✳ Chicas ✳ Girlies ✳ Glitter ✳ Strawberry ✳ Orange ✳ Blue ✳ Berries ✳ Kandy ✳ Street ✳ Rain ✳ Star ✳ Red ✳ Fluffy ✳ Ice ✳ Crew ✳ Posse ✳ Alert ✳ Gold ✳ Passion

✶ Girlz ✶ Pineapple ✶ Swirl ✶ Zoom ✶
Silver ✶ Attack ✶ Machine ✶ Killer

Just look at some of the names of other bands: Back Street Boys, Westlife, True Steppers, Atomic Kitten, The Cardigans, Blink 182. How hard can it be to come up with a name?

 Are you kidding – we hung around for days before we thought up anything that didn't sound ridiculous!

Well, yeah – it can be a bit of a pain, but it has to be done. But you can make it fun. When you have written down as many words as you can think of, put them all in a hat.

 Once the words are all in the hat, just take it in turns to pull one out and try it next to another word someone else pulls out. If it doesn't work straight away, at least you can have a giggle about how stupid you would sound with a name like PuffCorn or FunkyBerries. The first name we tried was GetFresh, which I thought sounded like a cure for bad breath!

Did you know...?

Hey – not all bands get their name right first time. Even solo performers have changed their original names to stage names to sound cooler. See if you can work out the original names of the ones we know.

a. B*Witched	Johnny and the Moondogs
b. George Michael	Pizzaman
c. The Beatles	The Tranzlator Crew
d. Destiny's Child	D-Zire
e. Fat Boy Slim	Girls' Town
f. Fugees	Yorgos Kyriacos Panayiotou

Answers

a. D-Zire b. Yorgos Kyriacos Panayiotou c. Johnny and the Moondogs d. Girls' Town e. Pizzaman f. The Tranzlator Crew

No wonder George Michael changed his name – imagine trying to say that without spitting everywhere...

PSST! Gossip H from Brit band Steps is really called Ian Watkins and used to get called Swotkins at school!

So that's it – you know what you're in for and you have your name – next you need some songs.

Rock on to the next chapter...

4.
Express Yourself

 Before you even think about choosing or writing any songs, you have to find out if you can actually sing!

Move your lips

Nearly all bands have a lead vocalist, so one of you needs to have a reasonably strong voice. Beyoncé is the strongest singer for Destiny's Child, and Jo and Rachel are the main singers with S Club 7. You'll notice that most bands tend to mime when on TV - but only because their dance routines are so hectic that they can't do both without passing out, *apparently*. Well, look at Britney and Madonna - they sing and dance at the same time, we are sure you can too! Try these top tips for improving your voice:

★ Stand up straight with your feet not too close or too far apart, your shoulders relaxed and your arms hanging lightly by your sides. Take a couple of deep breaths and clear your mind. This does take a bit of concentration!

★ To see what notes your voice can achieve, hum a low note and as you are humming start to speak a word in the same key as you are humming, like you're singing it. Hmmmmmmm-tomatoes... Or any word you like! Now try a bit higher doing the same thing, humming and speaking. Keep on going higher and higher until you can't go any higher or your voice sounds like a dying cat's! You should practise these all the time and you will notice the more you repeat them the higher you will eventually be able to reach.

★ Another way to make your voice stronger is to start with the humming, but this time open up the sound (very technical!) by singing the vowels from the alphabet: a e i o u. So try: Hmmmm-aaaaaa, hmmmm-eeeeee and so on, repeating from the lowest key to the highest you can reach.

Singing for real

In the second half of this chapter, there are ideas on how to choose songs and what to look for, but for now we need to concentrate on singing technique!

✦ You've got a song you want to sing as a group. If you're covering an old hit from another artist, really listen to the tune and see where the artist emphasises words while singing and try to copy that.

✦ You'll have to organize which one of you will sing which parts of the song and if one of you does have a stronger voice, they should really sing lead vocals, but that isn't a rule you have to follow.

✦ All of you should learn the words by heart, but to really get the melody in your head, sing it without the words (on a "la" or an "ooh" basis!). That way you learn how your voices fit together and you will also be aware of where the breaks are so you can take breathers – vital for strong singing!

✦ Practise, practise, practise – the most important piece of advice ever! Now you're ready to sing the words and the melody. Go with it, fill your head with the song and let go, so that what comes out of your mouth feels like the most natural thing in the world. And hopefully it will sound like it too...

> **Next up is songwriting. You may well groan inside and think it's all too much for you, but that's why we're here – to show you it ain't as hard as you think. Yeah! You all need to sit back and relax.**

Writing shouldn't stress you. It's fun! And you don't have to write your own stuff at first – give these ideas a whirl...

Music for wrinklies...

Now we know you laugh at your olds' choice of tunes, but they are worth sniffing out. Lots of girl and boy bands cover tunes from yesteryear. Westlife covered an old Abba slowie, *I Have a Dream*, and Samantha Mumba sampled *Ashes to Ashes* by David Bowie for her big hit, *Body to Body*. What you are looking for is something that has a catchy chorus and is basically very simple and easy to learn off by heart. Look out for stuff from the seventies and eighties - old disco songs are always a winner. Abba is always a brilliant band to copy and so are the Jackson Five - their tunes are so infectious and easy to make up dance moves to - in fact, S Club 7 sound a bit like the Jackson Five.

If you want to cover an old tune, find it in your parents' record collection and then club together and buy it as a Karaoke CD. That way you have the music and lyrics separately, so you can either add your own words or use the original ones from the song sheet.

PSST! Gossip Did you know that Tina from S Club 7 used to sing with Shola Ama before she nearly joined another band altogether? Phew – close call!

WWW.lyrics...

If you want to use other bands' lyrics but maybe add your own to them, that's also cool. If you want to cover a song that you heard in your olds' CD collection, but can't find the words – fear not! Look up lyric sites on the Net. This one is good: **www.lyrics.ch/index.htm.** Just about everything is on there, including chart music, so you can cover fave girl band tunes as well.

It's easy when you know how...

You might be feeling brave and try to write your own songs. But what do you write about? How about some pop star advice... Daphne and Celeste, mouthy US pop duo: *"Your songs should be about any kinda stuff – like your friends, your worst teacher or anything that makes you laugh."*

Hello – isn't that a bit clangingly obvious? Well, yes, but it *is* the best way to think about writing your very own songs. The Number One Rule about writing anything – stories or songs – is to write about what you know. The Spice Girls' first number one,

Wannabe, was about friendship. Daphne and Celeste's song, *Ugly,* was about bullying. Billie's first song, *Because We Want To,* was just about having a good time. So what do you know about?

Have a band pow-wow to discuss your "artistic direction"!!!! Pens, paper, Cokes and cookies are all vital ingredients to any serious song-writing venture. And then get to work.

Speaking as a professional songwriter myself –

Hey – we are all professional songwriters here!!

Yeah, Laydee, chill, I know. All I was gonna say was that unless you are all accomplished musicians and have instruments, the best thing would be to use the music of another song and just write your own lyrics. But of course, if you can play music, then go for it, girls! Or just sing without music, making sure the melody is a really strong tune.

PSST! Gossip Posh Spice on singing at home: "I can really go for it in the shower cos no one can hear me and if I sound like a cat then that's fine."

It's in black and white

So, back to getting those words down on paper. Write down words like this and see where they take you.

Friends	laughing	parties
	game	crying
dancing	playing together	bullying
	disco	sharing
falling over!		standing up for you
giving	loyalty	birthdays

Just writing down random words can spark off all sorts of ideas and start you on the path to that first song.

Once you've got some ideas, write them down. Pick a subject and choose a tune you want to go with, say Britney's *Baby One More Time*. Get a long piece of paper and count out the number of lines in the song. Then each of you takes a turn to write a line about the subject matter until you have a finished song. A really goofball way of writing is to fold over the paper after you have written your line so the next member of the band can't see. When you have finished the correct number of lines, unfold the paper and see what you've got. It might be total rubbish, but it might just be a stroke of genius! You never know. (Probably rubbish though, but at least it'll make you laugh!)

The chorus is really important when you're writing a song. You can make it rhyme, but it doesn't really matter. If you look at most song lyrics, they don't always rhyme. BUT - if you want to create rhymes, say if you're going to do a rap like LaydeeB, and you are stuck on a word, check out this web site: **www.writeexpress.com/online.html** - it's awesome! All you do is type in your word and press search and it comes up with a zillion words that rhyme with it. Cool!

And if you're going to be really professional, you need to write a bridge. It's a couple of lines just before the chorus, to connect the last verse with the chorus. You could write the bridge like a short rap.

Don't forget when you "sing" a rap, you don't actually sing it, you are speaking, but not like you're reciting a shopping list! You gotta give it some oomph and attitude and rhythm. Be bold, be loud and above all do it with confidence. You can see an example of bridges and choruses and how they work in our song, *We Say*.

We know girls who run and hide
But we can't do that
We got pride.
There's no point worryin'
What folks say
When all you wanna do is go out and play.

(Bridge)
Hey!
We're KandyFloz
Say!
Look who's boss.

(Chorus)
You wanna run with us
You gotta learn to be cool
Cos we are the girls who rule the school.
No one here can take our place
So come and join our funky space.

Don't be scared cos we don't bite
We just like
To give the boys a fright.
If they can't take it
That's just tough
We love to scare them with girlie stuff.
(Repeat bridge and chorus)
So girls, let's hang out
We got lots
To shout about.
We're closer than sisters
And that's the thing
That makes us wanna get up and sing.
(Repeat bridge and chorus twice to fade)

You don't have to start with the first verse – you can start with the bridge and chorus if you like. Or you could have the chorus repeated only once – it's totally up to you. But if you *are* following a well-known tune, you should keep to that song's structure .

We haven't talked about writing or reading music because that really is way too complicated for this book! Not all pop stars who do write their own tunes can read or write music, so we feel that for now, you can live in ignorance! What is important here is that you can at least sing and dance!

PSST! Gossip Oh no! Make sure you know all the words before you go on stage. Poor Nicole from All Saints forgot the words to *Never Ever* at a HUGE concert in Hyde Park, London in front of 100,000 people. We bet her face was cooking!

Now all you need to do is cut a disc, or rather tape yourselves singing your song, so you can see how harmonious you sound. Borrow a tape recorder and, if you can, a microphone and play your background music and give it all you've got. So — do you sound better than Britney and Christina?

If you want to have that true professional touch, make a tape cover for your recorded songs. Buy a throw-away camera and take pictures of all of you in stupid poses, get a grown-up to organise the developing, and then cut out your faces, the goofy poses and paste them on to a tape cover with a wacky design in the background and your name on there somewhere. Copy designs out of magazines – now you've got your first album!

5.
Dancing Queen

Hey! Get your boogie shoes on – we're gonna show those boy bands what we're made of! Don't worry, you don't have to do anything complicated – a routine only has to be a few moves to compliment the song you're singing. No need for acrobatics and swinging from the ceiling, we just wanna have fun and mess around to music.

I lurve dancing. But trying to get a routine together when Skye keeps staring off into space is infuriating.

Oi! Just watch your mouth, missy! I can groove.

Yeah, yeah. Well, here are a few tips from your resident shoe-shuffler and back-flip expert. Yes – *me*.

Kym's guide to not falling over...

✽ Don't try anything at all complicated at first. Make it as simple as possible and maybe when you get used to dancing together you can pull a few fast moves!

✽ If you are doing a slow number, dancing will look way over the top. All you need to do is keep moving on the spot in time with each other. Even just swaying from side-to-side is cool. Standing like a statue will look too weird. Just chill and go with the flow.

✽ Obvious – but make sure you're wearing shoes you can dance in. We don't want any accidents now...

✽ Check out all the videos you can to get ideas for funky moves. Watch as many Britney, Spice Girls, S Club 7, Steps and even those boy bands like Back Street and Nsync. They always have amazing dance routines, but remember they have been doing it for years and are superfit. You might end up in a sweaty heap if you try to copy and sing at the same time. Know your limits!

✽ Finally, when you're on stage and one of you forgets the exact move, don't just stand there like a lemon – everyone will be watching you! Make something up and try and get back in the routine as soon as you can. I remember Skye doing that on TV...

Will you stop causing trouble – no one noticed anyway. And my solo performance was better than those stupid steps anyway. Humph...

PSST! Gossip Billie Piper has a secret phobia: "Before I go on stage, I get really scared my shoes are gonna fall off... I have to tie them really tight, to make myself feel better."

Come on and move your body

So you've studied your vids and have an idea of what you want to do in time to your phat tune. Before you even start anything, have the singing all worked out so that when you do the routine, you can work around who is singing what bit of the song. That way, someone who is being swung round upside down and thrown in the air (get real!) won't be singing at the same time. Might get messy!

Here's my number one easy way to start a routine. All of you stand with your backs to the audience, with the person who starts off singing at one end of the line, then the rest of you following in order of who sings next. Turn round to face the audience one by one as you sing your bit until you are all facing the same way.

If you watch all the Billie and Britney videos, you'll notice one move that is a real favourite of theirs – the one-legged side shuffle. If you want it to look mega cool, you need to do it all in time.

Move 1

◆ Get your posse lined up with two in front and the other two or three behind, but to the side so they can be seen too.

◆ To make this easy, start off facing the front with both legs together and feet on the floor. Take a step to the right with your right leg and then bring the left leg over to join it like you are stepping sideways. Do that for four steps and then change and come back four steps to the left to where you started. That is all the move is, but funked up a little!

◆ Follow these instructions for the actual move in all the pop videos. Start by running on the spot at a steady pace – not so fast that you collapse from exhaustion before you've even started. When you've got a rhythm going, try dropping a little more weight on your left leg, so that it looks like you have a limp!

◆ Now as you drop your weight on to your left leg, move your right leg to the right, like you did when you were walking sideways. The minute your right foot touches the floor, bring your left foot over to join it so you have taken a sideways step to the right. When your left foot is on the ground, taking most of your body weight, move the right leg over to the right and repeat all over again.

◆ All the time, you are running sideways with your

left leg taking most of your body weight and your right knee kicking out to make those shuffle-hops across the stage to the right. Your hands can go on your thighs, or move like you are running with a very fluid motion.

◆ Summary: start, feet together – then step to right, bring left leg to join right foot, then step again to the right and bring left foot to join right one. Do this for about four beats across the stage and then change and go back the other way to the left, this time putting all the weight on the right leg and bending the left knee.

If you want a move to go straight after this one, have a go at this jump. When you have finished side-hopping, the two dancers in the front jump down on to one knee and lower their heads so that their foreheads are touching their knees. Next, the two girls at the back run towards them and leapfrog over them with their legs as wide as they can go. The minute the girls have jumped, the other two stand up and join them, ready for what's next.

Another quick way of moving in between moves: all turn out of your move and get into a line. Turn back-to-back with another member of the band to form two or three couples. Now side-step once right then left and repeat a couple of times together. A bit cheezy, but it can fill a gap in the routine.

Yeah, but you can also use that move for a more exciting one. . .

Move 2

◆ All stand back-to-back again in pairs and link arms with the person behind you.

◆ With arms linked, one half of the twosome bends over forwards-lifting the other one off the ground on to their back with legs in the air. The person bent over is taking the whole body weight of the other, so make sure you are equally matched for size! While up in the air on the back of your partner, keep one leg pointed and one leg bent.

◆ You can swap by lowering back down to the floor

quickly but still with linked arms, and then repeating it with the person who was supporting you. It will be quite hard to sing and do this, so perhaps do it when there's a break in the vocals.

This is one of the first moves we did as a group, and if done exactly in time it looks better than Backstreet!

Move 3

◆ All stand in a line with your left side facing the audience and about half a metre between you. Bend over forwards slightly so that you can touch your knees.

◆ Put your arms out in front with your hands out-stretched like you are going to clap. Then jump back about a metre, still bent forwards slightly, while bringing your arms back with you, closing your hands so it looks like you are grabbing something and pulling it. You can jump back as many times as you like – beware not to fall off the stage!

◆ To link this with another move or to jump the other way, when you have finished the final jump back, jump round to face the front and stand up straight, then jump round to face the other way and get in the position to jump back the other way. Sounds complicated, but it soooooo isn't.

 You can do lots of variations on this move. Instead of jumping back with your legs together, you could all stick one leg out in front and then alternate to the other leg when you do the next jump back. You can also do the move forwards instead of backwards and do different things with your arms. There are no rules. Just make it look funky!

 Hey! No one's mentioned the karate Sporty Spice kick! Jump up from your right leg then land on your left while kicking out your right leg out to the front. Girl Power!

Move 4

◆ Two of you stand in front and two behind but to the sides. Start running on the spot slowly to get the rhythm.

◆ In your head, chant, "right, left, right, left," when you land on the right or left leg, as this will make it easier to do the move. It's not a hard move to try, but this does help - honest!

◆ So - get down to the move! Start on your right leg, left leg, right leg and instead of landing on left leg again, kick it to the side like a karate kick. Hi-yaaaaaa! To go back the other way and kick the other side is soooooooo simple, even Skye can do it in her sleep. After you've kicked out the left leg, land on it and count that as left, then right, then left then kick out your right leg and back again until you get extremely bored and have to think of another move.

◆ Summary: right, left, right - kick left leg; left, right, left, kick right leg. Move your arms however you like - just keep balanced.

This kick can look funked up done as a routine, but kicking your leg to the side instead of to the front.

Ladies - don't use all your moves in one routine as it will look too busy and no one will know where to look. And also, you'll get so out of breath you won't be able to sing.

Yeah, these are by no means all the moves in the world, but I think you guessed that! The best thing is to make up your own by adapting what's here and what you see in pop videos – they're not hard to copy. That way, you should have enough for a zillion routines. Practise, practise practise!

6. Lipstick, powder and paint

It's makeover time. Get ready for an image overhaul and a whole new you emerging from what was once a shy and retiring girl. First of all, we are gonna take a peek at make-up and what a laugh it is.

What's in the bag...?

These basic items are what any girl band member absolutely cannot live without if she is to have that star quality look!

* Sheer coloured lip-gloss
* Glitter!
* Eye jewels
* Cream blusher
* Tinted moisturizer
* Pressed powder

* Nail jewels and nail varnish – all crazy colours are welcome!
* Gold bronzer for that Caribbean holiday look
* Eye gloss (or Vaseline if you are on a budget)
* Eye pencils in different colours
* Three-in-one colour pot or stick for lips, eyes and cheeks

So – what look you girls gonna go for? Individual looks like the Spices, or a similar group look like All Saints? Rude girls like Daphne and Celeste, or sleek and funky like Britney and Samantha Mumba?

You got the look

For make-up, what look you can carry off best all depends on your skin tone and eye colour. Here are some basic colour tips to get you started, cos you don't want to look like a horror movie now, do you?

Eyes...

Blue Eyes Try browns (they can make your eyes more blue); shades of blue, but not the same as your eye colour, and a shimmery white or lilac.

Green or hazel eyes Peach, mauve, shimmery gold, purple and silver all look great on you.

Brown eyes Shimmery golds and bronzes look great, as do stronger colours like greens and plums.

Lips and cheeks...

Fair skin Pinky-brown lipsticks and gloss and a warm pink blusher.

Asian skin Deep reddish-brown lips or deep purple-pink and beige blusher.

Medium and olive skin Deep pink or plum lips and peach-brown blusher.

Black skin Deep plum or brown lips and plum blusher.

 Now you know what colour should suit your skin, it's time to mix it up funky style with those make-up brushes and see what look suits you girls best. But first, you need to know the best way to slap on the new you...

Number one tip!

Always put on a tinted moisturizer first to give yourself a healthy look – you might be a bit pasty during those winter months. Make sure you rub it in carefully or you could look streaky! If you have a shiny nose, you might want to dab it with the pressed powder that should be the same colour as your skin.

Bat those eyes

✳ The secret of gorgeous eyes is not to cake eye shadow on. Even if you are using bright colours and glitter – less is more!

✳ For glamour eyes, sweep a shimmery shade over your lids, with a lighter shade, like silvery white, over your brow bone to highlight. Or you could try glitter.

✳ Eye jewels are the same as body jewels but smaller. Stick them on the outer corner of each eye with eyelash glue (not *real* glue – stupid! You don't want to end up in Casualty) if they are not self-adhesive. An alternative if you can't find eye jewels is to stick sequins on instead.

✳ For that dewy Britney look, blend a bit of your fave eye shadow with eye gloss or Vaseline and apply to your brow bone.

✳ If you are feeling confident, draw a line on your top lid with an eyeliner colour a bit darker than your eye shadow. Liquid liner gives a very hard line and is only recommended to those with a steady hand. Nothing is worse than that wobbly eye look. Oops… Better to use a soft pencil or an applicator brush to apply it instead. Gorgeous, baybeeeee!

✳ Finally – only use this if you promise not to poke it in your eye! Mascara will make your lashes appear thicker and stand out from the rest of your eye. Brush it on in upward strokes. Never do the bottom lashes unless you go for the panda look. Don't go mad and put a million layers on, either, or you will look like spiders are crawling out of your eyes. Euch!!!

Pinch those cheeks

★ For that sun-kissed look, lightly brush bronzer on the very tops of your cheeks by your eyes, on your forehead, chin and along the top of your nose. Now you'll look like you have come back from a very tropical video shoot!

★ Before you apply your blusher, pinch your cheeks to see exactly where you blush naturally.

★ Use your finger to apply the cream blush where your skin has reddened slightly and blend the colour gently, sweeping upwards towards the bronzer. Be careful not to drag the skin.

★ Glitter can glide along those cheekbones too.

Pout those lips

✦ Preparation is everything! Smear your lips with Vaseline and then rub an old toothbrush over them to get rid of flaky skin. Wipe it off.

✦ Apply a sheer gloss for a glamorous look with your fingers, making sure it doesn't bleed over the edge. Sheer means that the colour is not so strong as lipstick and looks more natural.

✦ If you are going to use lipstick, use a lip brush, as it will be easier to apply an even look without smudging. If you are going to gloss your lips, put extra gloss in the centre of both lips.

✦ If you can't afford lipstick and gloss, just cheat by mixing up your fave lipstick with a blob of Vaseline.

✦ You can even add glitter to your lips and go glitter mad, but don't have it on your cheeks and your eyes at the same time! Not very sophisticated, daaarling!

PSST! Gossip Beyoncé from Destiny's Child knows all about too much lipstick: "I had bright red lipstick on, and I didn't realise it had gotten on the microphone while I was singing. I was rubbing the microphone everywhere and got lipstick all over my face!"

All that glitters is gold !

Don't forget – you can add gold even when you have other colours on. It goes with almost anything. Highlight your cheekbones and brow bones, and put it on your lips too. If you want to look like a million dollars, when you have put on your outfit, dab gold body cream or highlighter on your shoulders and shoulder blades to shimmer like a star!

You've done your face, now you need to do your nails. A pop star has got to have nails to die for – so no bitten-down stumps for you. No way! Check out these top five tips for posh talons...

1. If your nails are too short (don't bite them!), you can press on false ones over the top to disguise them. But if you don't want to wear false ones, just paint a clear varnish on so you don't draw attention to them.

2. Use a good nail file to shape decent-sized nails – don't use a metal one. File in one direction only and do not use a sawing action – be gentle. Make sure your nails are clean before you paint them.

3. You are ready for varnish. Colours are up to you, but you can add nail tattoos under varnish and nail jewels on top of varnish – the varnish just needs to be wet so you can set the jewel or bhindi on the nail.

4. If you want to go for coloured varnish, apply with a very steady hand while your hand is resting on a magazine or something so it doesn't drip anywhere. Apply with one stroke on the centre of the nail and then one stroke either side to finish. Any smudges can be cleaned up round the edge of the nail with a cotton bud dipped in remover.

5. If you want to make a real splash, half-paint your nails one colour, wait for it to dry and then paint another colour to contrast. You could paint stripes of one colour on top of another. Paint a swirl on top of another colour after it has dried. Paint each nail a different shade, or with a fine paint brush, paint a letter on each nail to spell out words!

PSST! Gossip Britney bites her nails down to stumps! See – not everyone's perfect!

Luscious locks

Your hair is just soooo important if you are a pop star. Look how many times Madonna has changed hers, as well as Posh Spice going from mid-length to short to really long. You need to be able to keep changing – but how, without spending all your pocket money? Well... you could sweep your eyes over this collection of stunning styles that will make you stand out from the crowd and start setting new trends all over the world...

Hair accessories top ten:
1. Butterfly clips in different sizes
2. Hair bands in different colours
3. Kirby grips and hair slides with diamonds and flowers on

4. Spring beads or hair jewels (jewels on the end of metal coils)
5. Pony tail bands
6. Hair mascara
8. Gloss, gel and hair spray
9. Zigzag hair band (scrapes hair back from face)
10. Colour gel and glitter or colour spray

PSST! Gossip Did you know that Geri Halliwell's extensions came from several Filipino women and were dyed specially and woven into her own hair?

Plait attack

This looks really glam and different – good for on stage or a posh party. Obviously you have to have long hair. You will need to get some help with this one.

✴ Make sure your hair is really clean and slightly damp.

✴ Divide your hair into four or five sections, parting one section by your left ear and then working over your head to your right ear. Each section begins at your forehead and ends at the back of your neck.

✴ Start to plait at the front of your head, working backwards. The first part needs to be like a French plait, attached to your head with the rest of it hanging free. Then move on to the next section and slowly move across your head to your right ear.

✳ Once all sections are plaited, take the end of each plait and thread it through the top of another to make a loop. The loops should all cross over each other to make a pretty pattern.

✳ Use kirby grips to hold the ends in place, securing them close to the scalp.

Spiketastic

If you have short hair but it has a bit of length all over, this one will work for you.

★ Comb some gel through your hair – it helps if your hair hasn't just been washed.

★ Take a small section of hair and tie it in a tiny bunch with a band, then move on to the next section.

★ When your whole head is covered in tiny bunches, that's when you attack it with the hair mascara!

★ Backcomb the hair a bit if it isn't standing up (it should cos of the gel) and then brush the hair mascara on the spiky ends. You could also stick in hair jewels if you wanted to go completely over the top!

 That one's my fave!

Froth head

✳ Gather up the front of your locks and secure them with a butterfly clip.

✳ Tie back the rest of your hair and backcomb. Spray both sections with a bit of hairspray to give it a bit of hold – it should be full of volume.

✳ For the finishing touch, pin random strands of the backcombed hair loosely round your crown for that messy, just got outta bed look.

Poodle bunch

How do us girls keep our hair off our faces during those dance routines? Why, the poodle bunch of course…

✽ Take the front section of hair and pull it away from the face, towards the crown.

✽ Loosely twist the section a couple of times and secure it in a topknot using a ponytail band. Your hair should just fall over your shoulders.

PSST! Gossip Billie Piper's number one super-quick beauty tip is: "Let your hair dry naturally if you don't have time to dry it. Keep it behind your ears – that loose, wet look is in right now."

Do the twist

This looks better on shorter hair.

✦ Divide hair into sections, twist and fasten at the top of your head using glittery clips, butterflies or kirby grips.

✦ Backcomb the ends for a real spiky rock chick look and spray with hair spray. Now play air guitar!

✦ You could use a zigzag hair band and get the same result.

Quick fixes

✳ Short hair can be side-parted and pretty clips put in to keep the parting secure. Hair jewels can also keep hair parted – just slick some gel in first.

✳ When you plait hair, to make it look stunning, weave a string of leather or ribbon through the plait or plaits afterwards.

✳ When you put your hair in a ponytail, slick it back first with some gloss and then thread the end of a thin ribbon through a kirby grip and start weaving it across your hair from ear to ear. Do the same with two other contrasting coloured ribbons and tie the ends under your ponytail. Fab.

✳ Part long hair in the middle and tie each section into a high ponytail. Knot the ponytail in on itself, so it's like a bun. Then pin the knots to the side of your head with kirby grips while the pulled-through ends are left spiky.

✳ For rock chick big hair, plait long hair while wet and leave to dry or dry with a dryer. Undo plaits (you can do as many as you like) and separate with fingers. You can add hair jewels or clip a centre parting, and frizz out the rest of the hair.

✳ If you're sick of karma beads, use them to tie you hair back instead of a band – they look original.

PSST! Gossip Beverly Cobella, top hairdresser to all the stars, says that combing mayonnaise through freshly washed hair, leaving it for ten minutes and then washing, will make it shimmer with health! It does work – honest.

Right, that's all folks. Of course, now you have the hair and the make-up of a super-star, you're going to need the clothes from the catwalk to match.

I think LaydeeB has got some hot looks lined up for you in chapter seven. Rock on, babes! And remember what Daphne and Celeste say: *"If you're having a bad hair day, a cute little hair accessory can hide a multitude of follicular sins!"*

GIRL BAND

7.
Spice up your life

If you're in a girl band, it's important to wear the right clothes to get you noticed. Having a certain look that's yours is the way forward on the track to stardom. If you all look the same it can be boring, but if there's something that links all the band members, then that really works.

Now, sisters, you need the clothes and I am the LaydeeB to tell you how to get them at bargain basement prices. Discover a whole new you lurking in the back of your wardrobe!

Jean genie

"Denim is very versatile for the dance routines we do, and it's comfortable." Sinead, B*Witched.

Denim is the biggest fashion statement you can

wear as a piece of clothing because you can dress it up with posh shoes and sparkly jewellery or go casual with trainers and a sweat top.

Bleached beauties

So what clothes are the stars of the pop world sporting? Well, Destiny's Child, Britney and pint-sized star, Christina Aguilera, are all wearing bleached denims. And you can do the very same – all you have to do is ask mum or dad if you can transform an old pair. You might want to get some help from a grown-up, as bleach is nasty stuff and can burn you if it comes into contact with your skin.

✽ Wear really old clothes and rubber gloves so if you do splash it, it won't mater if it makes a mark. Do the deed in the bath – that way it won't make a mess.

✽ Make sure the jeans are clean and lie them flat in the dry bath. Pour bleach on to your jeans in a squirty pattern, not covering all of the blue – you want to still see some to contrast with the white. Turn them over and do the same to the back.

✽ You might want to just dye the bottoms of the jeans and create a gradual pattern up the leg, till there's no bleach at the top at all.

✳ Finally, when you've finished, you need to leave the jeans for a bit to let the bleach work. When the pattern has developed, that's when you wash them on the hot cycle in the washing machine. Now you have a pair of jeans that no one else will – true designer jeans!

PSST! Gossip Even pop stars have fashion disasters: "Once I wore this black body-suit and skirt. It was, like, really ugly. And the skirt was so tight it split when I bent over!" Beyoncé, Destiny's Child.

Super flares

 You ain't no one unless you got a pair of flared jeans – no girl band should be without a pair. I own at least five pairs. I know Fazza and Kym have a million pairs each. Feast your eyes here...

✤ Take an old pair of jeans that your mum won't mind you cutting up. Grab a pair of scissors and get a grown-up to help cut up the seam on the outside of each leg. Be careful not to snip the material, but just the stitching holding the seams together.

✤ Once you have unpicked about fifteen to twenty centimetres – stop! Sew over the ends of the thread where you have cut so the jeans don't unravel even more. Now you have jeans with a split up the side of each leg. You can leave them like this – they look cool – or go on to the next stage.

❖ Choose some cool-looking material – you can buy remnants in haberdashery stores, or maybe your mum has some lying around. Funky patterns, flowers, sequins, leather – anything that isn't denim!

❖ Stretch out the two seams you have just cut to decide how big you want the flares to be. Then measure the gap between the two seams and cut the other material to fit just over the area which will be the extra flare. You will need to hem the bottom of the material so it doesn't fray. Now sew the material between the two seams, sewing along each seam to disguise the stitches.

❖ Iron them and now you have a pair of customized mega-flares ready to do some serious dancing in. Karate kicktastic.

Easy stuff...

✳ Got a pair of jeans or trousers that look too plain? Draw a pattern on them in biro, round the pockets, bottoms, anywhere. Buy some pretty beads and sequins from a haberdashery store and get sewing, following the pattern you made. Beware! Only do small patterns, one at a time, as it can get very tedious sewing all those beads on!

 ✳ Jazz up a pair of old jeans with sequin trim. Just sew it on round pockets, down the sides of the jeans, or along the bottoms. Easier than individual beads.

 ✳ Fray jeans by cutting along the bottom and putting them through the wash a few times.

 ✳ Old trainers can be sprayed gold or silver and you can stick sequins on them for that over-the-top look you'll need for your stage show!

PSST! Gossip Christina Aguilera's top fashion tip: "When I'm not on TV or in front of a camera, then I always wear a bandanna. It helps hide the fact I haven't done my hair!"

Tight Ts

Tight T-shirts really are the secret to looking cool if you ask me. They look fab with baggy skating trousers, pencil skirts, jeans – just about everything. So do little vest tops. If you have some that you never wear any more – they've got a stain or you've just got sick of the sight – well, help is at hand...

 ✳ Dye old Ts different colours for each of you in the band. Get a grown-up to help.

✳ Draw out the name of the band, or your own names, on each T, then sew sequin trim round the letters and spell out your name sparkly style. You now look like the newest girl band to hijack the charts!

✳ Buy a cheap feather boa and cut it up and sew it round the necks, bottoms or sleeves of old Ts. You could do all three if you want to look like a real rock chick!

✳ Attack dark Ts with bleach like you did with the jeans – make sure they're cotton, though.

✳ Sew a shape on the front of your T in the same material as the flares in your jeans to make a whole outfit. Add sequins and beads.

✳ Wind sequin trim round the straps of old vest tops.

✳ Design a band logo on paper or on the computer, take it to a copy shop with your T-shirts and get it printed on the front.

✳ Sew a strip of Velcro on to a plain T and then cut out letters from some coloured felt. Make up your own slogans and phrases to go across the front.

✳ Get a grown-up to slash zigzag patterns with a sharp knife (eek!) in the front of old Ts and either leave for the dishevelled look, or sew funky material behind the slashes. Rock on…

PSST! Gossip Spotted at the MTV Europe awards – Madonna wearing a Kylie Minogue T-shirt held together with safety pins. Spotted at her first concert in years in the US – Madonna wearing a Britney Spears T-shirt. Spotted out shopping – Britney in a Madonna T-shirt. A new craze has been born!

 You girls might wanna wear skirts, and I haven't really mentioned them cos if you're a true girl band and you wanna strut your funky stuff, then dancing in a skirt is quite hard. You can adapt any ideas for skirts here, but remember – you won't be able to jump in the air gracefully without showing your knickers!

Accessory heaven

Don't get on stage without at least one of these:

* A headscarf to keep hair well out the way
* Karma beads to match your mood
* Beaded or feather choker
* Body jewels – look good when stuck on a midriff round the tummy button
* Silver rings, toe rings, thumb rings, fake tummy piercings
* Studded leather wrist cuffs
* Skinny studded belt or glitter belt

* Ankle bracelet, ear cuffs
* Fake diamond cross
* Chunky trainers, sandals or high boots
* Sunglasses
* Fake tattoos. Buy body art kits or henna tattoo kits so you can draw your own designs. Always follow the instructions. You could try some of these designs to paint on tummies and arms – even your feet!

PSST! Gossip Spicy Mel C might be regretting her tattoos: "When I first started getting tattoos I didn't even think, now I'm starting to panic how I'll look in twenty years." Go fake every time, we say!

Now you have everything – the make-up, the hair, the clothes – just put it all together and what have you got? Take a look and see...

Rock chick

Wears: Bleached flared jeans and cowboy boots or stiletto shoes, animal-print vest top and either leather funnel-neck jacket or bleached denim jacket.

Accessories: Fake tat-toos, diamond cross necklace, thumb ring, wrist cuffs and studded belt.

Hair: Spiky and short or a bright colour with ear cuffs showing.

Make-up: Glossy pink lips, bit of glitter on chest and lots of dark eye make-up with black-lined eyes and mascara.

Nails: Red with diamonds stuck on them!

Urban rap chick

Wears: Baggy hipster skating pants with pockets, chunky trainers, tight designer T-shirt, hooded sweatshirt and body warmer, and Kangol hat.

Accessories: Wraparound sunglasses, thumb ring, tattoos, funky watch, silver ring and ear cuff.

Hair: Chin-length style twisted into clips and butterflies, or zigzag hairband scraping it back from her face, and spiky at the back.

Make-up: Natural look with lip-gloss and a bit of brown eye shadow and mascara.

Nails: tattoos with clear varnish.

Slick chick

Wears: Tight hipster-style flared trousers or pencil skirt, high boots or strappy sandals and tight handkerchief top showing off midriff.

Accessories: Diamond cross, glitter belt, silver bangle, toe ring and ankle bracelet.

Hair: Either scraped back with spiky bits at the back, short and slicked back, or long and luscious with maybe a few highlights.

Make-up: Silver or gold eyes with another subtle colour to highlight, mascara, glossy pink lips, bronzed cheeks and shoulders, and maybe glitter too.

Nails: Natural with maybe a pink tinge or bhindis on the thumbs.

Hippychick

Wears: Frayed flared beaded jeans, gypsy-style top, chunky trainers or sandals and beaded cardigan.

Accessories: Feather choker, ear cuff, karma beads, bhindi, toe ring, ankle bracelet and tattoos.

Hair: Probably long, either in plaits or loose with jewels in it and, of course, a headscarf! If short, deffo hair jewels and butterfly clips.

Make-up: Pink or browny-red lips, pink cheeks, eye jewels and mascara.

Nails: Purple and silver nails with patterns on them.

PSST! Gossip Did you know that Britney has an obsession about buying sunglasses? She always buys a pair when she goes out.

You've checked out your basic looks. You don't have to stick to any style – these are just guides to help you get a look together. If you want more help, just check out magazines and watch TV – there's loads of info on fashion and style and gossip. Try these web sites for copying the looks of the stars: www.swizzle.co.uk and www.mykindaplace.com. Have you spotted me on there…?

PSST! Gossip Take a leaf out of All Saints Shaznay's book: "Don't wear clothes just because they're trendy. If you're not into what you you're wearing it'll stand out a mile."

8.
S Club Party

Now's the time for you to show off what you've been up to. Time for your public to see how amazingly talented you are and to witness your Out Of This World dance routines. It's show time!!!!!!

Party with the stars

Yeah, laydees, time for your showcase. Hmm… what's a showcase? A showcase is what all new bands have after a record company has just signed them. It's like a mini concert, but not so scary cos there are not so many people there - mostly music journalists from newspapers and magazines. Sometimes the showcase is so small they hold it in the studio where they recorded the album, so you could call it a party. All bands have had showcases - the Spice Girls, B*Witched, Westlife, Back Street Boys.

Edele from B*Witched says of her first show-case: "It was the most nerve-wracking thing I've ever had to do, but our families were there, so it made it easier." But you'll be having fun with all your mates – there'll be no nasty music executives to scare you off!

Lots of stars have lucky charms or rituals before they go on stage. Britney says a prayer and her... er... good friend, Justin from Nsync, puts pepper-mint oil under his nose to help him breathe easier! What would you do? Rub your lucky rabbit's foot?!

So how can you have a showcase? Easy! All you need to do is majorly grovel to Mum or Dad for use of the biggest room in the house – sometimes, the garage is better as it doesn't matter if you make a mess. As if...

PSST! Gossip You know you've made it big when your hometown wants to open a museum dedicated to you. Yes, you guessed it – Britney again! Residents in her hometown, Kentwood, are doing just that to celebrate her life.

Get bizzy with it

✶ Time to organize yourselves like an army of ants. Get those invites out: make sure they are glitzy with as much glitter as possible. Add stick-on jewels and bhindis so they look like individual works of art. You want people to get excited, don't you?

✳ Next is the room. You need it to look like the sort of place a band would have a showcase. A bit of glamour would be wicked, so you need to create an atmosphere. If it's in the garage, or the living-room, our top tip is to buy dust sheets from a DIY store. You are going to make the backdrop to your stage.

✳ Tuck the dust sheets over the top of the curtains at one end of the room so they cover them completely. If you're in the garage, see if you can hang them off the garage door.

✳ Have lots of card handy – now you are going to cut out stars and the name of your group and any other words in big letters. Spray the stars and words gold or silver and add glitter if you want (you know it makes sense!). Stick them on the sheets with double-sided tape.

✳ On the floor in front of the backdrop, mark out a rectangle with masking tape – that is your stage. Make sure you have enough room to do a routine. You don't want to fall off that stage now, do you? To add that special touch, borrow as many torches as you can and stand them round the edge of your stage area. Now how cool does that look when they're all switched on?!

✳ Hang stars and moons over the stage and/or whatever else you can think of. Use left-over stars and shapes that have been sprayed silver or gold on both sides and thread them on to pieces of see-through fishing thread – you can buy it in DIY stores – by making a hole in the top of each shape with a needle. Now attach them to the ceiling with tape, drawing-pins or Blu-Tak.

PSST! Gossip Stars sometimes have trouble on stage: Yonah from UK girl band Cleopatra once wasn't looking where she was going on the stage and slipped down the stairs on her bum in front of everyone! Embarrassing...

Now all you need is flashing lights for your show-case! You can hire them from disco and sound equipment stores, or a grown-up could buy them and keep them for other parties (they're not too expensive and you could ask for them as a birthday present). However, the cheap option would be to bribe little brothers and sisters to hold torches at the back and swirl them over the ceiling! Ho ho.

Rehearsing is vital. You need to know the limitations of the stage you have created on the floor and might have to adjust old routines to fit the space. You will also have made a tape from CDs of the songs you are to perform. Between each song, leave a couple of seconds' gap so you can catch your breath and get into the starting position for the next number. Make sure you have someone starting and stopping the tape for you so you're all on stage at the beginning – you don't want to be bothered with worrying about the music. Also, it won't look as professional. Remember to relax and do a few vocal warm-ups before you perform. Try the humming exercises from chapter four.

PSST! Gossip You don't want to be like Nicole from All Saints, who forgot to go on stage cos she was gossiping too much and missed her cue. She had no shoes on either!

 Right, that's it! You've sent out the invites but you can't just have a party about you, can you? You aren't Destiny's Child just yet, so you won't be able to keep your audience entertained for hours on end, will you? Well, no, BUT they could entertain themselves. Check these out...

Sing it back

You may be the only ones with a rehearsed routine, but everyone has a bit of pop star in them, don't they? You can bet all your friends do and they might be a tad jealous watching you strut your funky stuff on stage, so why not let them join in? Yes – beg, plead, do the washing-up for a week, even walk the dog in the rain, just so you can hire a karaoke machine! You know you wanna. What a laugh – watching your friends screech their way through *Baby One More Time* and out-doing drowning cats with tuneful renditions of *Bring it All Back*. If you can't hire a karaoke machine, buy one of the CDs, like the one you've used for your backing track, photocopy all the word sheets and buy a microphone that you plug into your stereo. Microphones are very cheap – just make sure your stereo has an output for one.

PSST! Gossip Jo from S Club 7's hobby is singing karaoke!

 To make it even more entertaining, have surplus accessories that the other "acts" can dress up in: feather boas, tiaras, hats, mad fright wigs or those hilarious Afro wigs (!) and a ton of body glitter.

Disco divas

Oh yes – that competition that always induces fights, squabbles and broken friendships! But it's worth it just to get on down and boogie. Have a dancing competition with prizes. The judge has to be someone not involved at ALL, like an older brother sister, parent, gran, etc. Everyone starts dancing in the style of someone like Britney or B*Witched and one by one, the judge eliminates everyone, until there are just two people left for a Give It All You've Got finale. Obviously, there are no rules, just that the best dancer wins. If you want to be in with a chance, check out the dance moves in chapter five.

PSST! Gossip US teen sensation Jessica Simpson's most embarrassing moment: "I auditioned for The Mickey Mouse Club and it was a disaster. I forgot every song – I might as well have been picking my nose!"

You'll all want to sit down after you've danced your legs off, so why not have a quiz to test your A-Z of pop knowledge? Try some of these questions, but it's really easy to make up your own from magazines and band websites on the Internet. You'll need loads more questions anyway, if you want your quiz to last more than five seconds!

Investigate some of these sites for star trivia.
Billie Piper, **www.c3.vmg.co.uk/billie;**
S Club 7, **www.sclub.com;**
Britney, **www.britneyspears.com;**
Spice Girls, **www.c3.vmg.co.uk/spicegirls;**

Backstreet Boys, **www.backstreetboys.com;**

Westlife, **www.westlife.co.uk;**

B*Witched, **www.b-witched.com;**

Steps, **www.stepsofficial.com;**

Madonna, **www.madonnafanclub.com;**

Destiny's Child, **www.destinyschild.com.**

For quiz questions and facts on up-to-the-minute bands, check these sites:

www.canwidecirculation.com/AllPop/trivi-afacts.html, www.dotmusic.com

Pop quiz

Split up into teams named after your fave girl pop band or performer and have a Quiz Master to read out the questions. Obviously, they can't join in. If someone knows the answer to a question, they have to shout out the name of their team first.

1. Which other teen queen started off as a Mousketeer on the Mickey Mouse Club with Britney Spears?

a) Mariah Carey

b) Christina Aguilera

c) Jessica Simpson

2. Give the FULL names of all five original members of the Spice Girls.

3. What is the name of Posh Spice's baby?
a) Brandon
b) Brooklyn
c) Birmingham

4. What is the name of S Club 7's TV show?
a) LA 7
b) NY 7
c) UK 7

5. Where did S Club 7's show used to be filmed?
a) Madrid
b) Miami
c) Montreal

6. Which country does Samantha Mumba come from?
a) America
b) England
c) Ireland

7. Name Christina Aguilera's first Number One hit.
a) Lucky
b) Genie in a Bottle
c) What a Girl Wants

8. Who are the twins in B*Witched?
a) Keavy and Edele
b) Sinead and Lindsay
c) Keavy and Lindsay

9. Which prince was supposed to have a crush on Britney?
a) Harry
b) William
c) Charles

10. Which famous pop diva did Westlife duet with?
a) Witney Houston
b) Madonna
c) Mariah Carey

11. Who is the youngest S Clubber?
a) Jonathan
b) Bradley
c) Hannah

12. Which Spice Girl had a chart topper with ageing rocker, Bryan Adams?
a) Posh
b) Mel B
c) Mel C

13. Who isn't a mother in All Saints?
a) Shaznay

b) Nicole and Natalie
c) Mel

14. Name the Spice Girls' third album.
a) Always
b) Forever
c) Goodbye

15. Which film did Destiny's Child sing the theme tune to?
a) Charlie's Angels
b) The Grinch
c) Stuart Little

 I could write out a million questions for you, but that's not the point! You have to think of them yourselves and create your own personal quiz. Don't groan – it's fun! Use these questions as a guide to the sort of questions you are gonna ask. See the answers below.

Get any right?

1. b 2. Geri Halliwell, Melanie Chisholm, Victoria Adams, Emma Bunton, Melanie Brown 3. b 4. a 5. b 6. c 7. b 8. a 9. d 10. c 11. a 12. c 13. a 14. b 15. a

There's loads of other stuff you can do at your show-case after you've done your thang. Get handy with that magic wand on your friends…

Celebrity make-overs

Transform your friends into the pop stars of their choice. Pile up those magazines and, using the make-up tips from this book, copy their looks. Britney is all dark eyes and lots of eyeliner, with pink lips and sparkly eye-shadow. She says her fave eye shadow is brown, with a dark brown on the lid and a lighter one brushed on her brow bone. Posh goes for maximum make-up coverage with glossy lips and eyes as her trademark and VERY tight clothes. B*Witched always look casual, with glitter for glamour, but don't forget their uniform of denim. Now, who wants to be Madonna…?

Who am I?

After you're all made up, you can play the ridiculous guessing name game. Sit round in a circle and each of you write down the name of a pop star on a Post-It note and stick it on the head of the person next to you, making sure they don't see who it is. Each person has to ask a question to the group about the person they are (am I a girl? am I in a group?) If they guess correctly, they get to ask another question. If not, the next player has a go. The winner is the first person to guess who they are. And, yes, you do all look stooooopid with those bits of paper on your head!

PSST! Gossip Did you know that so many celebs sell out and endorse all sorts of stupid products? Britney has a hair accessory, bum/fanny pack and doll, Christina has her own self-adorned lunchbox, and the Spice Girls had their own dolls and Cadbury's chocolates with their signatures on the wrappers!

Have a cocktail party! All showcases have nibbles (in pop star circles they are called canapés, dahling) on trays handed round by waiters – you wanna look like true stars, dontcha? Get a grown-up to help you out with the food side of things. Give these canapé ideas a whirl: mini sausage rolls, tiny cucumber sandwiches with the crusts cut off, cheese swirls (see recipe below), tortilla chips with salsa and sour cream dips, mini spring rolls (you can buy them ready made), pizzas cut up into neat squares. Basically, the word here is MINI. As long as it's small and you can fit it in your mouth in one go, it can be a canapé! You might have to bribe younger brothers and sisters to hand round food like those posh waiters...

Cheese swirls

This is a yummy party food and soooo quick to make. You will need help with this from a grown-up.

Roll out a pack of store-bought puff pastry till it's about half a centimetre thick. Grate enough strong cheese to cover the whole area of pastry and then roll it up into a sausage. Now slice off discs of pastry and place them on a greased baking sheet. Bake in a medium oven till they are golden brown. You can make pizza swirls by spreading tomato paste on the pastry before you add the cheese. Ta-da – yum!

Cocktails

If they're having a showcase, most bands drink champagne, but you're too young. Doh! BUT, you can have fruit cocktails instead. Deffo need the grown-up help here with the blender – don't try and work one yourself. For strawberry cocktails, whiz some strawberries in a blender and add to orange juice with loads of ice. For a banana surprise, mash a banana with blended strawberry and mix with milk and vanilla ice-cream. There are loads of combos you can do – orange and banana; coconut milk, orange juice and strawberry; banana, cranberry and orange juice; Coke and orange juice (!). Just experiment before you try them out on any of your friends – you don't want to poison them.

PSST! Gossip Britney loves making cocktails. Get a grown-up to whiz vanilla ice-cream and soft fruit like strawberries or bananas in a blender and experience a Britney Smoothie! Hannah from S Club 7 has a fave smoothie recipe: five strawberries, a banana, orange juice and a scoop of ice-cream all blended together for a cool S Club cocktail.

You've got loads of action planned for your showcase party – enough to keep everyone amused. The main thing to remember is to give it all you've got while performing and have a scream. You are entertaining your audience and yourselves!

GIRL BAND

9.
A star is born

We all started somewhere and we've just given you your start on the road to fame and fortune... well, an idea for a pretty cool party, anyway. How do you think your favourite pop stars burst on to the music scene? Was it overnight, or was it after years of hard slog and sweat, singing in grotty clubs and bars? Well, why dontcha look and see...

All things nice

Why don't we begin with the one and only Spice Girls? They are (fingers crossed) still together, but rumours fly round everyday that our fave girl band is about to call it quits. Maybe they will, maybe they won't, but here's how it all started...

Posh, Ginger, Baby, Scary and Sporty all met as far back as 1993 at various unsuccessful auditions for singing and dancing jobs, and ended up sharing a house in Maidenhead, Berkshire in the UK. When Simon Fuller took them on as manager in 1995, they had already started writing songs and making demo tapes. A record contract with Virgin swiftly followed and by June 1996, their first single, *Wannabe,* was on its way to number one in the UK. By February 1997, they had made it to number one in the US, making history as the first UK act to make the top of the American Billboard with their debut album.

Towards the end of '97, they sacked their manager, Simon Fuller, and everyone thought they would sink without a trace. Oh ye of little faith – it takes more than that to break the Spices! To prove their popularity, their movie, *Spice World,* was released on December 26th 1997 and became a monster hit all around the world. The number one singles kept coming as did the Spice Dolls, chocolates, jewellery, T-shirts, books … you name it, there was a Spice Girl with it! But suddenly something awful happened just before their world tour: Geri left the band! How were they going to cope without their Girl Power leader? Well, just fine, it seemed. Life went on and they continued their world domination with a sell-out tour, coming back to Britain to rest, have babies (Posh and Scary), get married (Posh and Scary!) and do solo projects (Sporty and Scary). It looked like they might split, but no – the new millennium saw a more grown-up Spice Girls (not sure that's such a good thing) with the release of their third album, *Forever*. This started a famous battle with boy band Westlife in the UK charts, ending up with both bands declaring chart and personal warfare on each other. Now, that's not very lady-like, girls! The Spice Girls are still going strong at the moment, but for how long, with all these up and coming teen stars ready and waiting to steal their crown?

Take a leaf out of Destiny's Child's book and work really hard to get to the top. The younger you start (they were only nine and ten!), the easier it will get later on with all that experience behind you. Did you do the quiz in chapter three? Could you handle school and singing and dancing every day till you make it big? Check this out...

Independent women

Destiny's Child is the BIGGEST Girl band in the world at the moment. Go girls! They had a number one single, *Independent Women Part One*, on both sides of the Atlantic in December 2000. However, the trio, consisting of Beyoncé Knowles, Michelle Williams and Kelly Rowland, didn't used to have the same line-up as they do now. The Destiny's Child story began in 1990 Houston, USA, when friends Beyoncé and LaTavia Robertson hooked up with Beyoncé's cousin Kelly Rowland, and spent afternoons studying videos of the Jackson Five and the Supremes to mimic their dance routines. Two years later, LaToya Luckett joined the group and, with the final member in place, the girls found they had a special chemistry.

Coming up with a cool name was proving tricky, but fate intervened. One day, Beyoncé's mother picked up the Bible and a picture fell out with the word "Destiny" in the title. They adapted this to Destiny's Children and then shortened it to Destiny's Child.

Armed with their fab new name and Beyoncé's dad acting as their manager, the group kick-started their career with a performance on the US talent show, *Star Search*. The girls were pitched against acts nearly three times their age, and while they didn't win, it certainly got the ball rolling. LaTavia recalls the show: *"We were kind of nervous about it. They made us do a rap song, although we wanted to sing."* Gradually, low-profile appearances in and around Houston led to Destiny's Child supporting bigger and bigger acts when they came to town. By 1996, the group had signed to a record company and all those years of hard slog had finally paid off when their first single, *Killing Time,* from their debut album, appeared on the soundtrack to the Will Smith film, *Men in Black.* Their second album in 1999 was a massive seller and from there on, they climbed to dizzy heights with many hits, including *Say My Name, Bills, Bills, Bills* and *Jumpin', Jumpin'.* Now mega-stars, award winners and famous all over the world (and still with an average age of eighteen!), the group faced a crisis point in March 2000. LaTavia and LaToya left the group, but were immediately replaced by nineteen-year-old Michelle Williams and eighteen-year-old Farrah Franklin! That's the pop music merry-go-round for you! Well, after five months with Destiny's Child, Farrah also quit! And this is where we end up ten years later (!) with the talented trio we know and love – our kung-fu-kicking funky angels that are storming the charts and carrying on in the Girl Power tradition. We salute you, Destiny's Child!

See – you can do it too. Entering competitions is the way to go if you are serious about wanting to be famous. Just make sure you can sing! Singing into the bathroom mirror is a good start, just like Britney used to when she was five years old...

Mickey Mouse paves the way...

So how did the Britney Spears phenomenon kick off all those years ago? *"When I was a little girl, I was always performing. I remember buying* Thriller *[Michael Jackson's album] and I used to dance around the room all the time."* From as far back as she could remember, Britney had always wanted to sing and dance and attended dance and gymnastic classes. Aged nine, Britney learned that the Disney Channel was holding auditions for *The Mickey Mouse Club*. Britney shone like a star when she met the producers, but she was deemed too young to be a Mouseketeer and was pointed in the direction of an agent instead. Soon after the audition, Britney, her mum and her little sister Jamie Lynn left the safety of their town Kentwood, Louisiana, to move to rough neighbourhood Hell's Kitchen (eek!) in New York to help nurture Britney's artistic talents. While there, every summer she attended the Off-Broadway Dance Centre and the Professional Performing Arts School and was soon landing parts in TV adverts and Off-Broadway shows. Like Destiny's Child, she also entered *Star Search,* but Britney won!

At eleven, Britney was now old enough to reapply for *The New Mickey Mouse Club* and she landed a coveted spot of a Mouseketeer. As well as Britney, there were other Mouseketeers with bright futures: Christina Aguilera – and JC Chasez and Justin Timberlake both from Nsync. It was during her time on *The New Mickey Mouse Club* that Britney realised she wanted to pursue a career in music. After two years, Britney handed back her Mouse ears and returned to Kentwood for a normal year in high school, but was soon wishing she were off travelling the world performing for audiences. Britney decided to audition for girl group, Innosense, in a bid to achieve her dream as a pop star. As usual, she stood out for being so brilliant (go, Britney!), but the manager of the group wouldn't take her – he thought she was too talented! For real! He sent Britney's demo tape to Jive records, where they immediately saw her potential and offered her a record deal.

After recording her album in Sweden, Britney came home and was sent on a national tour of shopping malls, like Debbie Gibson and Tiffany had done in the eighties. But instead of becoming a one-hit wonder, Britney was mobbed everywhere she went and when she brought out her debut single in 1998, *Baby One More Time,* there was Britney mania! She had a hit all over the world and her album of the same name was also a mega success internationally. It was the start of the Britney rollercoaster. Her second album, *Oops!... I Did It Again!* was released in 2000 and Britney commenced a world tour for the first time. All this and only nineteen years old! This just proves that teens continue to rule the school!

PSST! Gossip

So, you now have an idea of how much hard work being a pop star involves. Do you still want to do it? All stars have similar stories of gruelling tours, initial poverty, no privacy and not much sleep. Madonna only had $37 in her pocket when she arrived in New York to make it in the record industry. She was reduced to eating leftover fast food from bins when she ran out of money! Farrah Franklin was rumoured to have left Destiny's Child cos she couldn't cope with their full-on schedule. Other pop stars had very unglamorous jobs before they made the big time: Keavy Lynch from B*Witched worked as a car mechanic before she joined the group, and Geri Halliwell was a game show hostess on a really bad Turkish TV show. But if you wanted fame badly enough, you'd be willing to put up with all these things and do anything, wouldn't you...?

That's all our advice on everything you need to know about being in a girl band. So that's it. Remember to keep practising those routines and have a laugh. We all had to start somewhere and now you know how some of the biggest stars in the galaxy made their way to superstardom. We want to hear good things about you! And if you make it big, don't let them make those Barbie dolls of you — they always look way uncool!

10. Knowing me, knowing you

Right, you've been given loads of advice and heard about everyone else out there playing the fame game, dancing the dance, talking the talk and wearing the latest clothes. But what about you? We don't know anything about you! We wanna know!

Girl Band Press Release

Fill in this section of the book and keep it as a souvenir of your time in a girl band.

Your band name

_____

Members of the band

_____

_____

_____

_____

_____

Your band picture

Your favourite song you perform

_____

Your most embarrassing moments in the band

_____

_____

_____

_____

_____

_____

Where was your first performance?

_____

Have you had any pop star bust-ups yet?

_____

_____

_____

List your favourite outfits

_____

_____

_____

_____

Trainers or shoes?

_____

_____

If you could film a pop video anywhere in the world, where would you go?

_____

_____

What would you have in your dressing room at a concert? Eg. pizzas, Coke machine, personal slave, etc!

_____

_____

_____

_____

_____

_____

Who are your top five favourite bands or pop stars?

_____

_____

_____

_____

Which pop stars should be banished to outer space?

_____

_____

_____

If you could record a single with anyone, who would it be?

_____

_____

Name the best-dressed pop star ever

_____

Backstreet Boys or Nsync?

_____

Neither! Girls rule!

Name your top ten songs of all time

_____

_____

_____

_____

_____

_____

_____

_____

_____

_____

Name your top five worst!

_____

_____

_____

_____

 Last bit of advice before the end of the book – practice your autographs! It took me ages to perfect mine. You never know when someone will ask you to sign, or what they will want you to sign. I heard Edele from B*Witched had to sign a nappy for a fan! Hope it hadn't been used.

Good luck and have fun with the book. Try not to fall over on stage and all will be cool! We know you are going to be BRILLIANT! Byeeeeee!

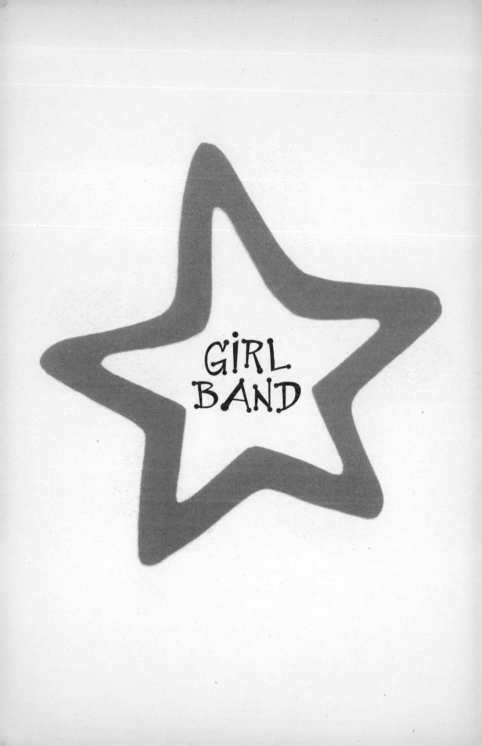